HERALDIC DESIGN

ITS ORIGINS, ANCIENT FORMS
AND MODERN USAGE,
WITH OVER 500 ILLUSTRATIONS

HUBERT ALLCOCK

DOVER PUBLICATIONS, INC.
MINEOLA, NEW YORK

Acknowledgements: The helmets on page 25 are redrawn from Franz Sales Meyer, *Handbook of Ornament*, as are the shields on page 32. The arms of the American republics were furnished by the Pan American Union, Washington, D.C.

Bibliographical Note

This Dover edition, first published in 2003, is an unabridged republication of the work originally published as *Heraldic Design: Its Origins, Ancient Forms and Modern Usage* by Tudor Publishing Company, New York, in 1962.

DOVER *Pictorial Archive* SERIES

International Standard Book Number: 0-486-42975-X

Manufactured in the United States of America
Dover Publications, Inc., 31 East 2nd Street, Mineola, N.Y. 11501

CONTENTS

INTRODUCTION

ERALDRY has become through the centuries the exact art and science of the herald, as law has become the art and science of lawyers, and medicine that of the physician. Today's world is well acquainted with both physician and lawyer, but the professional term *herald* is little known. Professionals in this field prefer to be called heraldic *artist, expert,* or *researcher*. The United States army, for example, has a heraldic office; its chief, of course, holds military rank and is not called the Army's herald. Such groups as the National Genealogical Society in Washington *do* have officials formally termed herald — but these are elective posts and the incumbents are not required to be professional armorists. Today, in fact, the only professional heralds who function in anything approaching the traditional sense are those appointed to their official posts by the British Crown or the government of the Irish Republic.

But arms and symbols appeared on the battlefields — and elsewhere — long before heralds came to serve any role in society. From the earliest stages of man's development, groups and individuals have used signs or marks for identification — symbols that we call *emblems* or *insignia*. Emblems in general are older than man's ability to read and write; men of all cultures and times have used them. At first the system of emblems was simple and functional: they appeared for purposes of identification and, in the earliest times, with the intent of frightening the enemy (as in the first illustration at the top of page 10). The system of emblems introduced by European knights during and following the Crusades was much more elaborate, and later periods saw a growing complexity. The development at its most extreme grew from the simple to the downright silly, as can be seen from the sequence illustrated on page 9. The more disciplined evolution of symbols is shown graphically by the progression that appears at the top of pages 10 and 11.

The emblems shown on the shield were known

first as *cognizances* and were later called the insignia (ensigns) of the arms, or simply *the arms*. Confusion in terminology was compounded by the fact that both the shield and the coat of arms (the tunic) invariably carried the same emblem. The flag bore the same marking as the tunic and shield, and knights also adorned the tops or *crests* of their helmets with yet another emblem of a similar nature.

Although military units had long used flags for identification and regrouping purposes in battle, we cannot be sure whether these flags were transferred onto the shields or whether the shield emblems were fresh creations born of necessity. Each knight carried a shield but, like a lance, it could be lost or broken in conflict. The tunics or "coats of arms" were the safest and most spectacular aid to identification, but only the term *coat of arms* (wrongly applied in most cases) survived the age of chivalry.

Shields (or coats of arms) began to assume the prestige of their bearers and their usage was extended as artistic embellishment symbolic of the nobility of the possessor. Arms were carved in wood and stone, impressed in metal, and appeared almost endlessly in castles and churches, on monuments and tombstones. They were embroidered into tapestries and worked on rich garments. Most frequently of all, they appeared on coins and seals.

At the same time, the shield was being adopted as a background for the emblems of many who had never borne arms in battle — clergymen and scholars, artists and craftsmen, merchants and notaries, burghers and even peasants. It became the custom for churches, universities, guilds, and cities, as well as for families, to display armorial bearings. Thus, although the ancient battle shield had disappeared, its image lived on, deeply ingrained in the imagination, tradition, and culture of European society. Despite the appearance of other emblems — badges, knots, and impresses — arms maintained their central and official position as the permanent emblem of any given group.

Bartolus de Saxoferrato (1313–1357), the author of the first treatise on arms and other insignia, defined the essence of arms when he compared them to family names, for family names are also emblems, inherited in a way somewhat parallel to that in which arms are inherited — although with the succeeding generations of professional and free-lance heralds, the inheritance of and the right to display arms became more and more complex, governed as they were by the growing body of heraldic stipulations.

With the increasing popularity of arms, it became clear that there was a need to record and control armorial bearings. The heralds did not initiate the compiling of arms in rolls of Honor Arms, but eventually they did take over the whole business. Since they were the only ones with accurate records of who had adopted what emblem, they became the powerful and controlling advisors to those persons who wanted to adopt new arms. At the same time they further developed the language and rules of blazonry, which gave them still stronger control of armorial rights.

Apparently the so-called Holy Roman Emperors began the custom of granting arms by giving their own family arms (with some changes, of course) to individuals and families they wished to honor. Emperor Charles IV, who was also king of Bohemia, granted Bartolus — for example — the Bohemian lion with changed colors, as a sign of his favor. Being a lawyer, Bartolus quite approved the idea of a grant of arms by a ruler because he recognized the advantages of a solemn and public adoption of arms. In an age that had no copyright agency, the only way to let people know one had a particular arms was to publish them in some other form. The royal grant was ideal for the purpose, as legal as a will drawn up before authorities. Though not necessary for validity, the publicity would prevent contesting possession of arms. Although Bartolus recommended a grant of arms, he maintained that any family, common or noble, could adopt and rightfully use arms without the benefit of such publicity.

Bartolus admitted that duplication of arms, like that of family names, was possible. He was also aware of reasons for *not* duplicating arms and felt that they should be copyrighted like trademarks and hallmarks — making priority an important factor. Out of this basic idea grew the widespread feeling that one should avoid taking another family's arms and (an idea certainly not discouraged by colleges of heralds) obtain official permission before adopting any at all.

Another notion restricting the free display of arms at first was that only nobles, knights, and gentry could rightfully possess them — a natural outgrowth of the fact that originally only the sons of the upper class were eligible for knighthood and consequently participation in tournaments. Commoners raised to nobility automatically got a grant of arms; from this practice grew the opinion that "ignobles" had best refrain from using them, another opinion the professional heralds did not discourage. In spite of the heralds, monarchs continued to grant arms (with or without nobility) as they saw fit or as whim dictated. In actual fact, a considerable number of arms adopted in every region were never granted by anyone.

In Britain, some — afraid to use arms without paying for them at the College of Arms — employed crests instead. Unlike arms, crests have never been regarded as copyrighted. In Scotland, a clansman had the privilege of wearing the crest and motto of his chief as his badge, and — since belonging to a specific clan came to be based on family name alone — any Macdougal or Morgan could use any Macdougal or Morgan crest he liked. In a similar fashion, many families of British extraction adopted the crest of the most prominent family bearing the same name. Others, with neither the same name nor a perfectionist sense of heraldic rules of the game, borrowed the crest of a family with a similar name. To this crest was gradually added the full achievement — including arms and motto; this seems to be the origin of the current popular misuse of the term *crest* for a family achievement. These misappropriations and abuses are of comparatively recent origin.

The Bayeux Tapestry, one of the most authentic sources of information on the Norman invasion of England in the middle of the eleventh century, shows detailed scenes of the Norman conquest on an embroidered band of linen more than 230 feet long. Fascinatingly accurate in every aspect, this tapestry shows the type of armor that was worn and the kinds of shields the knights carried — but nowhere on it does there appear a coat of arms, credible evidence that such devices (even if known) were not used at that time.

During the course of the next century, however, the open-faced helmet was discarded in favor of a closed helmet, and articulated plate armor superseded chain mail. With the combatant completely encased in steel, an instantly recognizable device became essential for the distinguishing of friend from foe. The pattern chosen by the knight was simple and forceful, for one very good reason: so that it could be recognized without margin for error at a distance.

The appearance of heralds and troubadors is closely connected with that of the true knight — or, more precisely, with the transformation of the mounted warrior into a more sophisticated class of fighting man: the knight. The gallant and violent games the knights developed to keep themselves in combat condition evolved into exciting and exacting contests, becoming with time an elaborate and popular form of public entertainment.

Games of chivalry apparently could not take the field without managers, umpires, announcers and

One path of heraldry — from powerful through ornate to silly.

Left: the shield of Edward II (1307–27). *Center*: the leopards from the earlier shield reappear in the Tudor "achievement" and remain in the modern English royal arms (p. 30). *Right*: a parody of poor contemporary commercial art with a misapplied royal garter (bearing a motto which can be roughly translated "It is easy to imitate what someone else has initiated"), excessive use of coronets, and a helmet out of which no one could possibly see — or, for that matter, could have gotten into in the first place. (The formal motto on the scroll is "Things are not what they seem.")

other functionaries any more easily than can organized sports today. Announcers or heralds were enlisted from the group of wandering showmen (troubadors included) who earned their livelihoods by furnishing entertainment in village squares and manorial halls.

The original function of the herald, then, was to serve at tourneys much as sports commentators do today. The pomp these specialists exploited became known as heraldry. They blazoned (called out) the insignia of participants, proclaimed their titles, recited their battle victories, and noted their standing in the lists. In this period of development, heralds and heraldry were connected solely with pageants and not with armorial bearings and other emblems that came to be associated with their functions later. As time went on, they became more and more the autocrats of the blazoning board, prescribers of ritual, and *chefs de protocol*.

Heralds had nothing to do with the adoption of cognizances by knights, and in the formative era they did not control the elaborate system now called "armory." But in their role as callers-out — blazons — of the insignia of individual knights, they doubtless created the techniques of describing (or blazoning) these insignia in a precise technical language. This unique language of blazonry, which reduces every emblem and its components to an unequivocal descrip-

tion, enables artists to recreate or "emblazon" any arms from its description alone.

Heraldry's first theorist, Bartolus, does not mention heralds. Nor does he speak of quartering or marshalling. This can be interpreted either as his rejection of the complication of simple arms or — what is historically more probable — as the fact that in Bartolus' time the symbolism of armory was still simple.

At the end of the eleventh century, the First Crusade introduced a new setting and a new type of warfare that was to affect Europe for the next three centuries. Vast armies took up the sword to champion Christianity; new heroes emerged from the battlefield and new arms were blazoned for posterity. The new conditions, moreover, provided a new source of artistic inspiration for the busy heralds. The cross naturally figures prominently in many of the heraldic designs of this period; numerous secular symbols also worked their way into the arms of the time, of which so many signified the triumph in the Holy Land.

The restless adventurers from England, in their travels to the East and in their contact with both Greeks and Saracens there, came in touch with a different civilization, in many facets much more refined than their own. Far more than new motifs for arms, they brought back new habits and ideas that contributed in large measure to the great revolution of

the Renaissance.

The fourteenth century was the golden age of *chivalry*, the spirit and customs of knighthood, the gentler spirit of an age filled with coarseness and brutality. Its ideals were high, though the practice was frequently hollow.

In the first year of his reign, Richard III incorporated the heralds, forming the College of Arms that continues today. The College of Arms consists of thirteen members: three kings of arms, six heralds, and four *pursuivants* (those who pursue a skill, knowledge, or an art; as this term indicates, they must achieve some heraldic mastery to warrant their appointment).

In England today, heralds form the College of Arms; in Scotland the Lyon Court. Ireland has its own chief herald.

Following the Age of Reason and the Age of Enlightenment, the revolutionary spirit of the nineteenth century and the tag-end of the eighteenth saw a considerable public aversion to the display of arms. The republicans of the French Revolution, for example, regarded arms as so tainted with the prerogatives of nobility that they forbade them. They abolished the Arms of France — and no subsequent French Republic has ever again adopted them.

The American colonists and revolutionaries, however, included a good many individuals who displayed their arms proudly. George Washington, when he was adding a second story to Mount Vernon in preparation for his marriage to Martha Custis, wrote his agent in London to send along his coat of arms; he had it painted on his coach and it appears in at least two places in the architecture on the main house at Mount Vernon. John Paul Jones was awarded his personal arms by the King of France.

The new Republic devised new arms for the Union and for the individual states (see pp. 78–86). The poor quality of some of these devices owes something to the contemporary aversion to traditional heraldry which helped bring about the general decline of the art, which reached its lowest ebb at just this time.

After the French Revolution, a wave of anti-armorial sentiment hit America, too. Suddenly arms were considered undemocratic and snobbish. People forgot that the Union, as well as the states, had arms. Seals, on which arms most frequently appeared, were for some reason not involved in this negative attitude and began to serve the function formerly played by arms. Thus today most people are familiar with the Great Seal of the United States but do not realize that the Arms of the Republic exists separately. Many cannot distinguish between the two; others ask what difference it makes whether we use one or the other.

One by-product of this confusion is the fact that entire seals are often displayed on flags, rather than the arms alone, cluttering them with unnecessary detail and making easy recognition difficult. (An outstanding exception to this is Maryland, whose state flag properly displays only the arms handed down from the Lords Baltimore.) The complete Great Seal appears on our paper money, but our coins and stamps have no arms to identify them. Even the President and Vice-President of the United States speak from platforms adorned with their seals rather than their arms. All these current uses ignore the original design and function of a seal — which was to be affixed to a treaty or a deed, to confirm an action or to secure an envelope.

When popular interest in family arms began to revive during the nineteenth century, an attempt was made by many to find an emblem that could somehow demonstrate the family's importance, noble origin, or possible royal blood. Since no newly adopted arms could serve this purpose, frantic hunts were launched for ancestors who had been granted arms in earlier times.

There are, in fact, no purely "American" arms.

Those that are accepted, in the strictest heraldic sense, are all basically European arms, "matriculated" by the existing Colleges of Arms in Europe. The contention of this book, however, is that a return to the simple heraldry of the Age of Chivalry is desirable and that there is no reason not to design one's own armorial bearings, following the sound principles of the earlier heraldic ideal.

Well-designed armorial devices, flags, badges, and seals still have a place in this nation. Not all of the state governments possess what can truly be called arms, and many of the existing official emblems could well afford redesigning. This is also true for various governmental departments, the branches and divisions of the armed forces, and a multitude of patriotic and social-service organizations.

Only a few U. S. universities have arms worthy of note (see pp. 87–88). Most high schools have make-shifts that are dreary and often in poor taste, although they do exhibit school colors, a carryover from heraldic tinctures.

The flags of today's organizations beg for the services of the specialist in armorial design. Compare the practice of covering these with elaborate, over-designed, heavily lettered insignia with the beautiful and elegant flag of the Red Cross. Churches, too, could benefit from armorial devices that would identify them distinctly.

The improvements that could be achieved in corporation trademarks are legion. (see pp. 40–42). Traditional dignity, good taste denoting solid establishment, uniqueness of design with greatly increased display and recognition value are all possible if correct heraldic practices are followed. Monogrammatic gimmicks would then give way to graceful designs of beauty.

Too many designers today admire and continue to copy the decadent abuses of the Baroque and Rococo in heraldry. It is often claimed that the client insists on such practices — and many do.

There are other individuals who prey on the ignorance and vanity of people who want arms to display. These opportunists compile lists of families of the same name and offer the prospect a picture of "his" arms. These charlatans should simply be avoided like the proverbial plague, and anyone who wishes to establish his own right to the possession of arms should take special care to obtain information from a thoroughly reputable source.

Good heraldry can flourish in America as it does in Europe. The commercial designer can contribute by following the laws of good heraldry to be found in this book; the general reader can contribute by informing himself what good heraldry is and by insisting on nothing less than the best.

HUBERT ALLCOCK

A good example of an American armorial device, redrawn from the seal of the Ohio Company. The tilting helmet is correctly proportioned to the "heater"-shaped shield. The supporters are authentically costumed, easily identifiable as (dexter) a Plains Indian and (sinister) a Five Nations Indian. The beaver crest symbolizes industry; beaver was also a principal trade item. Three stags *statant reguardant* form a simple and easily recognizable arms. The motto states the Company aims — *Peace and Commerce*. (Note that the torse and mantling, as shown, are not part of the original seal. They have been added here only for the sake of completing the components of an achievement.)

The Ohio Company was formed in 1748 by London businessmen and Virginia planters led by Thomas Lee. Chartered in 1749 by George II, it was granted 500,000 acres west of the Appalachians and south of the Ohio, with the stipulation that 100 families be settled and a garrison maintained. Between 1749 and 1754 many storehouses were built and the surrounding country explored. The French and Indian War caused the settlers to flee in 1756 (the Five Nations were allies of the French) and an otherwise successful venture was abandoned.

After the Revolution another company — the Ohio Company of Associates — was formed to purchase the land between the Ohio and Lake Erie. Congress voted the sale of 1,500,000 acres to the company and granted additional plots free. The company was unable to pay in full, but a large tract was bought for nine cents an acre. The town of Marietta, Ohio was settled in 1788 and colonization and development proceeded at a rapid pace. This second company was headed by Rufus Putnam and Benjamin Tupper, both of whom were New Englanders.

Crest. Figure or symbol affixed to top of helmet, usually derived from arms.

Torse. Wreath; two skeins of twisted silk, one tinctured as principal metal, other as principal color of arms; used to anchor mantling to helmet.

Mantle. Cloth worn over helmet as protection from sun. Repeats principal color of arms; lining repeats principal metal.

Helm. Authentic helmet style, size reasonably scaled to shield. Helmet follows position of crest (frontal or profile) in sensible relationship. Naturally colored steel helmets considered proper.

Shield. Heart of the arms; design is exclusive, may not ethically be imitated. Design of shield should be simple, easily recognized, and unique with bearer. Basic divisions or plain fields with repeated charges are most effective. Rules of heraldic tinctures always carefully followed.

Supporters. Originally decorative, now emblems through usage and association; reserved for those in authority, titled families, governments.

Compartment or **Ground.** Legitimate when there are supporters to stand upon it. May represent turf or be decorative "gas bracket."

Motto. Not considered exclusive. Usually Latin; expresses ideal, goal, or admonition.

The shield is the heart of any armorial bearing and — with its tinctures, charges, and ordinaries — makes up the basic arms. The stylized heraldic shield is the surviving counterpart of the actual weapon of defense traditionally carried on the left arm by warriors through much of human history.

Battle shields were originally of wood, metal, or of hide stretched over a wooden or wicker frame. Phoenicians, Trojans, Greeks, Romans, Vikings, Saracens, Crusaders, and Highland Scots were among those who used the round shield first developed in the Bronze Age. Roman legionaries carried the oblong, convex wood-and-leather shield called *scutum* — the word from which *escutcheon* is derived.

So far as we know, the kite-shaped Norman shield was the earliest bearer of heraldic cognizances; a representation at Le Mans of Geoffroi Plantagenet (*ca.* 1150) shows him with a shield of this type that displays golden lions on a blue field. The Norman shield was shortened after 1200 and the rounded upper corners squared — a shape that, as a result of the elasticity of its curves, became the best form for the display of heraldic arms.

Widespread use of the cross-bow made shields useless as protection; after about 1360, warriors began to discard them as battle equipment, although tilting shields continued to be used in tournaments and pageants, reshaped according to function or the whim of the bearer. Armorial artists, too, began to reshape the shield to fit architectural or decorative requirements and to follow the style of the time; by the Rococo period they were often scarcely more than decorative plaques, far removed from their military ancestors.

The nineteenth-century revival of romantic interest in chivalry led the Victorians back to the "heater" shape, so called because of the general resemblance of this shield to the outline of the flat irons then used in the laundry. Since that time the trend in heraldic design has continued, at least in shield outline, to keep the Gothic simplicity — evidenced even in commercial emblems (see pp. 40–42).

A woman, incidentally, does not properly display her arms on the shield forms used by men; the code prescribes the oval (more rightly, the lozenge) to show her paternal arms (if unmarried) or her husband's and those of her father (if married or widowed).

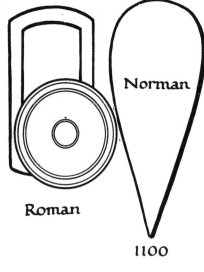

Roman

Norman

1100

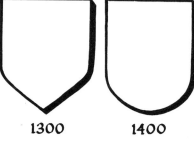

1300   1400

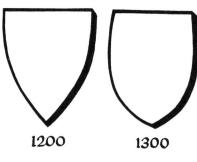

1200   1300

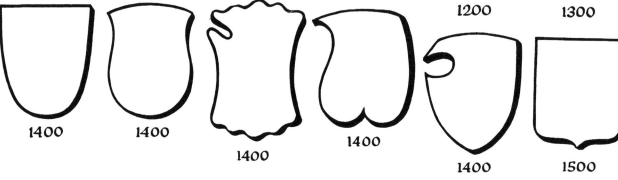

1400   1400   1400   1400   1400   1500

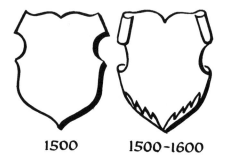

1500   1500-1600

Various Oval Forms

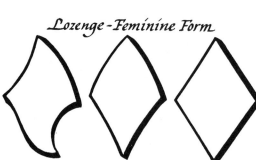

Lozenge-Feminine Form

Tincture is an important term in heraldry; for simplicity, consider that it covers colors, metals, and furs. Color is essential in armory, particularly in bearings and flags; designs that are similar in black and white may be quite different in their correct heraldic tinctures.

The colors in heraldry are illustrated here; common names follow the heraldic ones. (The traditional names are medieval French; blazonry [see page 29] never uses the modern equivalents.) *Purpure*, seldom used on shields, appears on crowns and mantlings. In black-and-white reproduction, as here, an arbitrary system of *hatching* represents each color — a scheme which tradition attributes to a Jesuit priest.

Heraldic metals are *or* (gold) and *argent* (silver). When a blazon calls for gold or silver, flags substitute yellow or white; artists often substitute in similar fashion. (Aluminum is used instead of silver on permanent hand-renderings, because it does not tarnish. Gold does not tarnish, therefore either gold leaf or pure gold water color can be used. Gold-bronze with a tempera or lacquer base soon turns brown and so is useful only temporarily.)

Furs in heraldry are traced to the covering of shields with the skins of beasts. Common furs include ermine and its derivatives, *vair, counter-vair,* and *potent* (the Chaucerian word for "crutch") — which may have developed from badly drawn *vair.*

A universal rule of good heraldry is that *color shall not be laid upon color, nor metal upon metal* — a heritage from the days when instant identification of individual arms was vital on the battlefield. Therefore the shield whose *field* (background) is a tincture must have upon it an ordinary or charge that is metal, and vice versa.

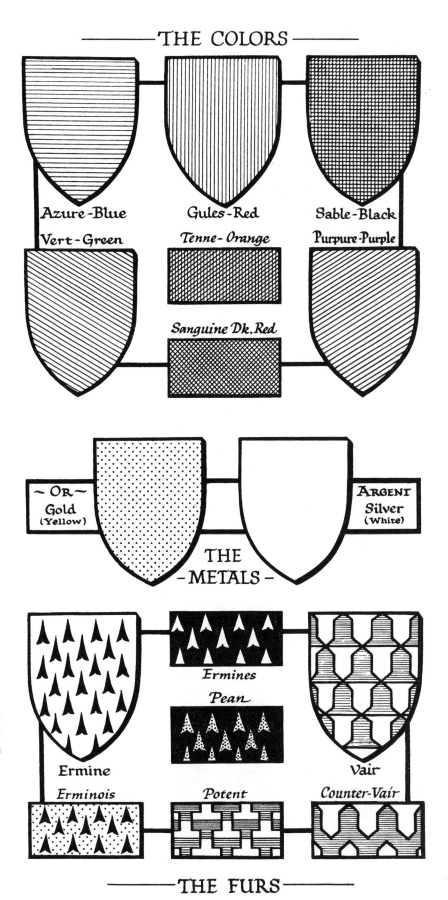

— THE COLORS —

Azure - Blue Gules - Red Sable - Black

Vert - Green Tenne - Orange Purpure - Purple

Sanguine Dk. Red

~ OR ~
Gold
(Yellow)

ARGENT
Silver
(White)

THE
— METALS —

Ermines

Pean

Ermine *Vair*

Erminois *Potent* *Counter-Vair*

—— THE FURS ——

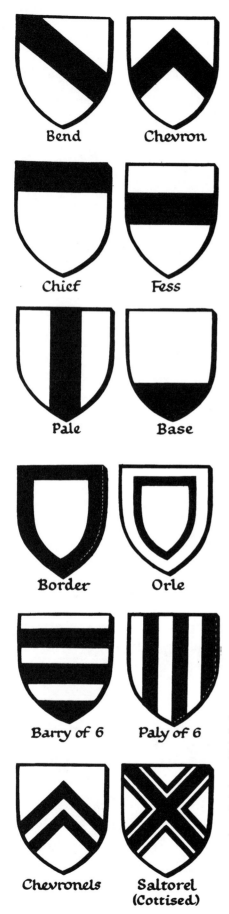

Bend   Chevron

Chief   Fess

Pale   Base

Border   Orle

Barry of 6   Paly of 6

Chevronels   Saltorel (Cottised)

Shields were originally plain or of one tincture; then they were divided by vertical, horizontal, or diagonal lines intersecting the center. The resulting sections were of contrasting tinctures. This limited the variety of possible combinations, so **charges** (figures or designs) were overlaid — "charged" — on the shield to create new and distinctive arms. Charges are of a tincture or metal different from that of the field. The simplest charges are bands or stripes, called **ordinaries**, following the vertical, horizontal, and diagonal divisions. Ordinaries have their own *diminutives* half their width: bendlet, chevronel, bar, palet, and saltorel. A shield divided into six bars is a *barry of six*, into six palets a *paly of six*.

Use of the cross in arms became popular during the Crusades; only a few of the many varieties that were developed are shown here. The cross of Lorraine is also known as the patriarchal cross, the tau as the cross of St. Anthony, the saltire as the cross of St. Andrew, and the saltorel as the cross of St. Patrick.

Tinctures reversed on either side of a partition line are said to be *counterchanged*. The counterchanged shield shown to the right is described as per pale argent and sable, a chevron counterchanged (see Blazonry, p. 29).

At times rulers grant an *augmentation* to existing arms as a reward or honor. The bend on the Howard arms bears a shield resembling that of Scotland (see p. 31) awarded for slaying the Scottish king, except that the lion here is a demi-lion.

Scottish sovereigns have granted the *royal tressure* to families (including the Kennedys) and cities (among them Perth).

Saltire   Cross

Latin   Tau

Lorraine   Papal

Maltese   Fleury

Counterchanged
Chief Wavy   Chevron

Howard Augmented   Royal Tressure

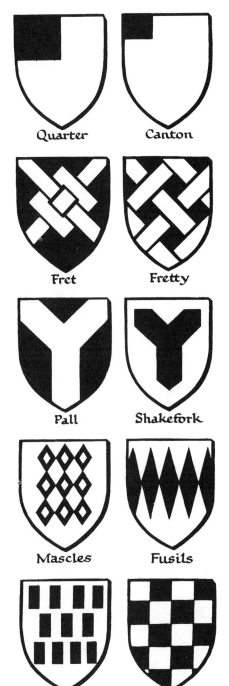

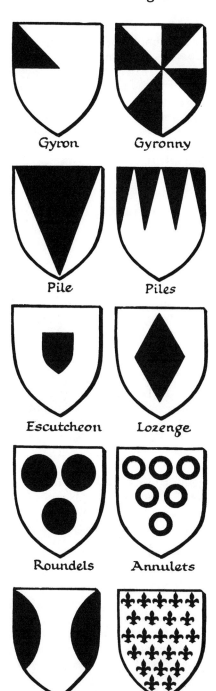

There exists among the ordinaries a large group all of which tends toward greater complexity than is normally found in the common ordinaries. These are called by some the **subordinaries.** Of the frequently found patterns, only a very few are illustrated here.

In many ancient arms, it was the practice to try to relieve the plain surfaces of the field by covering them with a repeated ornament. This process is called **diapering,** a process that is to be found in many other areas of decoration and adornment, from wallpaper and textiles to parquetry and metalwork. In heraldic usage, this serves the purpose of surface decoration only and can never properly be employed in contrasting tincture or in any other manner that would allow it to be mistaken for a charge.

It is not always the case that the **lines of partition** that divide various portions of the shield are rendered straight. Eleven of the many kinds of line commonly used for this purpose are shown and named in the box at the lower left.

In describing arms, there is a standard scheme that is followed for **division of the shield.** In determining left-and-right designation correctly, this pattern is based on the shield as seen from behind — that is, from the position of the warrior who held it. Accordingly, the *dexter* (right) of the shield is always to the left as we look at it. Conversely, the *sinister* (left) of the shield is to the observer's right.

LINES OF PARTITION

Engrailed
Invected
Embattled
Indented
Raguly
Dovetailed
Potenty
Nebuly
Wavy
Dancetty

DIVISIONS OF THE SHIELD

1· Dexter Chief Canton
2· Chief Point
3· Sinister Chief Canton
4· Dexter Flank
5· Center Point
6· Sinister Flank
7· Dexter Base Canton
8· Base Point
9· Sinister Base Canton

Shield divisions and ordinaries make up the simplest arms, but the many possible variations of these were far from exhausted when knights added to their own arms other devices, the so-called **common charges** that include, among hundreds of others, the examples shown and described on pp. 18-24. Animals, particularly the lion, were displayed by the earliest bearers of heraldic arms.

During the Crusades some real monstrosities stalked into this bestiary; these exotic creatures are still seen in heraldry.

The heraldic antelope and tiger are both particularly remote from their living prototypes. The **antelope** here resembles a stag with straight horns, short nose tusk, tufts of hair on chest and neck, and a leonine tail. It is *statant* — standing on four feet. The **boar** was, in contrast, well known in Europe and hunted for sport, so part sufficed for all, and the boar's head here is *cabossed* or *caboshed* (Fr. *caboche*, head, cabbage) or "headed" to the onlooker, no neck visible. The **bear** is a popular city and family emblem in Europe. Two bears (or other animals) may be *addorsed*, turned back to back.

The **cockatrice**, shown *erect* (upright), was a monstrous serpent with head, legs, and wings of a cock, and a "death-dealing eye." The **deer at gaze** *statant* looks straight at us, regarded from the next shield by an English **dragon**, a ferocious monster with scaled body, wings, claws, long barbed tongue and tail. (French dragons look like the English wivern.) Beasts of prey and monsters are usually shown reared up on hind legs, right foreleg uppermost; unless otherwise blazoned, the term *rampant* is assumed.

The **griffin** is a monster with forepart of an eagle and hindquarters of a lion. A rampant griffin is termed *segréant*. The **fox's head** is characteristically *erased*, torn from the body — apparent from the jagged neck. Heraldic **fleece** is the

Antelope,
Statant

Boar's Head
Caboshed

Bears,
Addorsed

Cockatrice,
Erect

Deer,
At Gaze

Dragon,
Rampant

Griffin,
Segreant

Fox's Head
Erased

Fleece

Lion, Rampant-
Guardant

Lion,
Rampant

Lion,
Queue-fourché

Lion, Rampant Tail Nowed

Male Griffins, Combattant

Paschal Lamb

Pegasus, Courant, Gorged

Sea Lion, Reguardant

Sea Horses, Regarding

Talbot's Head Couped

Tyger, Sejant

Tyger, Sejant Erect

Tyger, Sejant Erect Affronté

Unicorn, Passant

Wyvern, Erect

full pelt of a ram — head, horns, hooves, and all.

The **lion** is, with the cross, the most popular of charges. Lions are always shown *rampant* and *dexter* unless otherwise noted. A lion *salient* (similar to rampant but with both hind feet on the ground) has a *nowed* (knotted) tail. Two lions or monsters may be *combattant*, facing each other in fighting stance.

The **Paschal lamb**, a symbol of Christ, stands supporting with its right foreleg a staff in bend sinister from which hangs a white flag with a red cross.

Pegasus sprang from the body of the slain Medusa. Winged or not, a horse is often shown *courant* (running); any animal with a coronet about its neck is *gorged*.

The **sea lion** has head and shoulders of a lion, fins for paws, and the tail of a fish for a body. The **sea horse** is half-horse, half-fish. Any animal looking backward is *reguardant;* its head is thus turned toward sinister or *contourné.* Two animals facing each other but not combattant are *respectant* or *regarding.*

The long-eared, heavy-jowled **talbot**, probable ancestor of the bloodhound, is usually white. His head is not erased but *couped*, cut off in a straight line. The heraldic **tiger** (the Asiatic tiger is portrayed striped) has a natural tiger's body but the head of a dragon, although the tongue is not barbed. (Animals may be pictured *sejant*, sitting down with forelegs erect, or *sejant erect,* sitting on hind legs only with body erect and forelegs extended. A beast normally faces *dexter.* Facing the onlooker, it is said to be *affronté.* A tiger so shown in actual armory is unique; lions in this position are much more usual.)

The **unicorn** is portrayed as a small, vigorous horse with one horn in the middle of its forehead.

The **wivern** is a fierce cousin of the cockatrice and the dragon and appears a composite of **the two.**

Crane,
In its vigilance

Eagle,
Displayed

Eagle,
Rising

Eagle,
Close

Eagle,
Double-headed

Falcon,
Jessed & Belled

Martlets

Owl

Pelican,
In her piety

Phoenix

Wings,
conjoined in Lure

Bee

The **crane**, tradition says, lived in a community in which individual members took turns standing watch. The sentry crane held a stone in one claw; if it dozed, the falling stone would awaken the bird. A crane is thus commonly emblazoned "in its vigilance," right claw holding a stone.

The **eagle**, king of birds, rivals the lion for frequency of appearance as a heraldic charge and is usually shown *displayed* (wings spread). In this position, birds other than those of prey are said to be *disclosed*. Less frequently an eagle is *rising* (taking wing) or *close* (wings closed). Double-headed (*bicapitated*) eagles were both Sumerian and Hittite symbols. Theodoros Laskaris was the first eastern Roman emperor, Sigismund the first western to use two-headed eagles, a usage continued into the twentieth century by Austrian and Russian emperors.

The hunting hawk or **falcon** is traditionally shown *close* to avoid confusion with the eagle, which it resembles. Falcons are often *belled* with hawk's bells or *belled and jessed* and are also blazoned *hooded*. (Jesses are leather binding straps; a falcon hood is a tufted blindfold.)

Martlets, originally martins or swifts, are often shown without feet and sometimes without beaks. The **owl** has long been a symbol of wisdom. Heraldry's **pelican** is usually emblazoned as a mother bird standing over her nest and feeding her young with drops of blood plucked from her breast; she is thus termed "in her piety" (compare the Pennsylvania Dutch *distelfink* on p. 38). The **phoenix** of ancient lore, is shown as a demi-eagle *issuant* from flames.

Falconers fastened together a pair of wings as a training lure; **wings** are thus always emblazoned as *conjoined in lure*.

Symbolic of labor and thrift, the **bee** is no stranger to shields.

Differing from today's fighting man, knighthood often chose flowers — symbols of purity and beauty — in preference to lions or dragons.

Heraldic plants rarely appear complete on shields. The representation stresses some significant part; the leaf or flower shown from above reveals its components. The **cinquefoil**, for example, is the leaf of the Potentilla divided into five leaflets, a motif frequent in Gothic architecture. The **garb** is a sheaf of grain. Its binding cord and the "ears" may vary in tincture, but garb is usually gold over-all. Similar in origin to the cinquefoil, the **quatrefoil** has four cusps.

The **rose** is shown from above, only the bloom and its parts visible. Five fully opened petals are usually shown, *barbed* and *seeded*. *Barbed and seeded proper*, a rose has green barbs and gold seeds. Two branches of the Plantagenet (Sprig-of-Broom) family that ruled England adopted red (Lancaster) and white (York) roses as badges. The War of the Roses (1452–85), resulted in annihilation of the entire family and victory for the Welshman Henry (VII) Tudor; he combined the pretenses of both branches with the Tudor rose, five white petals inside, five red outside. This Tudor rose, *slipped* (stalk added) and *leaved*, became the plant badge of England.

In heraldry, the tree stump is a **stock**; it may be *couped* (cut off) and *eradicated* (torn up by the roots). A complete tree may be emblazoned on a shield, leaves and fruit drawn disproportionately large. It is thus *fructed* or (if in bloom) *blossomed*. The **trefoil** is a three-lobed leaf, possibly clover, of Gothic origin.

The **dolphin** is always shown *embowed*. The overlords of Dauphiné used it as their emblem as early as A.D. 830; *dauphine* became their title and an embowed azure dolphin their arms. Fish have long appeared in heraldry; their usual positions are *naiant* and *hauriant*.

Cinquefoil

Garb

Quatrefoil

Rose, Barbed and Seeded

Tudor Rose

Rose, Slipped and Leaved

Stock, Couped and Eradicated

Oak

Trefoil, Stalked and Slipped

Dolphin, Embowed

Pike, Naiant

Salmon, Hauriant

Caltrap

Castle

Castle Triple Towered

Chess Rook

Crescent

Clarion

Decrescent

Increscent

Escallop

Escarbuncle

Estoile

Fleur-de-lis

Inanimate objects further enrich armory's variety of charges. Many of the man-made objects in heraldry are associated with warfare. A **caltrap,** four short spikes conjoined so that one point is always up, was a device to maim an enemy's horse — and the ancestor of a similar present-day antitank weapon.

It is also quite natural that the **castle** is a frequent heraldic emblem. A castle may be drawn with two or three towers, and is blazoned accordingly. A castle of another kind is that from the ancient game we know as chess. The heraldic chess rook, however, does not resemble the rook with which we play today; it looks like the piece formerly known as the archer. The **rest,** also known as the **clarion,** may be considered either a lance rest or a form of wind instrument.

The heavenly bodies are familiar charges, with the **moon** mistress of the field. The proper tincture of the moon is argent; the most frequent form is the half moon with horns upward, blazoned *the moon in her crescent.* With horns sinister, the moon is *decrescent;* with horns dexter it is *increscent.*

Among the fauna we have the **escallop** or scallop shell, badge of pilgrims to the Holy Land. The **escarbuncle** is a survival of early shield ornamentation. It consists of eight decorated iron bands or staves radiating from a central boss. **Stars** are among the oldest emblems and are found in heraldry in many forms. The traditional star of old English and French heraldry was the **estoile,** usually six-pointed, always wavy. The five-pointed star that appears on the American flag is a derivative of the mullet (p. 23) on the Washington family arms.

Much has been written about the origin and significance of the **fleur de lis,** but the question is still unsolved. To some it is a stylized iris or lily; others consider it an ancient religious symbol identical with the *trisula* — trident and lotus. The **lymphad** (Gaelic *longfhada*, long ship) is a vessel fitted for both sail and oar. The **maunch** or **manche** is a Gothic sleeve with a hanging lappet. The *fer de moline* or **mill-rind** is an iron clamp that supports the millstone. In early times this apparently indicated the bearer's *millsoke*, a duty imposed on his tenants to grind their grain in his mill only (and pay him a fee for the privilege). Twelve Miller families in England have been found bearing a cross moline and none a millrind, suggesting that this may have evolved into the cross moline.

The **mullet** looks like a five-pointed star. Its French name, *molette*, shows it as the rowel of a spur. Shown *pierced*, it is often referred to as a spur-rowel. The **pheon** is an arrowhead of ancient origin. It was made of fine steel, barbed and engrailed on the inner edges, making extraction difficult. Pheons are more common in traditional heraldry than entire arrows and bows.

The origin and meaning of the **palmer** or **pilgrim staves** is evident. A **portcullis** was a grating of metal or heavy timber, armed at the lower edge with great iron spikes, sometimes suspended over the main gate of a castle to be dropped on pursuers. A **seax** (Old English, knife) or **sax** is a short, broad single-edged sword or dagger of Teutonic origin. On English shields it appears, rarely, as a *falchion* (broad-blade, slightly curved sword) with a semicircular notch at the back of the blade.

The **sun** is always proper or *in his glory* (*splendor*) emblazoned as a golden disc surrounded by a number of rays (usually sixteen) either wavy or alternately straight and wavy, issuant from the circumference. *Eclipsed*, the sun is emblazoned sable. The disc usually shows a human face. The **tower** is as common as the castle. The **water bouget** represents pigskin bladders for carrying water, on a yoke.

Lymphad

Maunch

Millrind

Mullet

Mullet, Pierced

Pheon

Pilgrim Staves

Portcullis

Seax

Sun In Splendor

Tower

Water Bouget

Human figures are frequently found in heraldry as supporters (see p. 13). The full-length figure is comparatively rare on the shield itself, one well-known exception (not shown here) being that of Munich — a cowled monk *affronté,* arms extended.

Parts of the body are often found as charges; the arm, cubit arm, hand, leg, and heart are familiar armorial devices. The forearm or **cubit arm** is usually erect. The **arm,** couped at the shoulder, is generally *embowed* or *counterembowed* (bent with hand turned dexter or sinister). Either may be *vested,* clothed (in tincture different from that of the sleeve), and on occasion *belled* (jester's cuff). The hand is ordinarily *erect appaumé* (palm to front) and couped at wrist.

The **human head** is customarily *affronté* and couped at the neck. If bearded, the neck may be hidden, as in the head of a Saracen, wild man, or savage.

Islamic heads (Saracens, Turks, etc.) often have a torse-like scarf around the temples, blazoned in alternating tinctures. Hair and beard are usually sable. The head of a wild man or savage is wreathed with vegetation, hair and beard uncut and shaggy, expression fierce or angry; figure is naked and muscular, loins girded with vegetation. He may carry a massive tree bough as a club.

The **mermaid** is a glamorous half-woman, half-fish, a favorite crest emblem of seafarers. She is almost always emblazoned holding a mirror and combing her hair. Her male counterpart — merman, **triton,** or Neptune — is bearded and armed with a three-pronged trident. He may be crowned or wreathed with seaweed and girdled with marine plants.

Gutté, representing drops of blood, milk, tears, and the like, occurs frequently in heraldry as a background texture.

Arm Embowed Cubit Arm Cubit Arm, Vested & Cuffed

Hand, Appaumée Head Affronté Mermaid

Saracen's Head Savage Triton

Gutté d'or Gutté de sang Gutté de poix

The **crest** is the highest ornament of a shield of arms. Its origin is probably more ancient than that of any other of the heraldic bearings — Homer describes the "crested helms" of Greek and Trojan warriors. The right to wear the crest was held in highest esteem in the early days of heraldry because crests could be acquired only by those who had seen actual service in the field as knights.

The crest is properly displayed only upon a helmet. Since similar crests are common, inclusion of the tinctured torse, mantling, and motto tie it definitely to a particular family.

The popular misuse of the term "family crest" in place of the more correct "arms" is traced by some heraldic scholars to the old right in Scotland of any member of a clan to display his chief's crest as his badge, leading to the practice of using crests by those without just claim to regular arms. A crest alone cannot be awarded to anyone unless he possesses arms — thus, without a shield no family can claim a crest.

The Crest

Helmets in heraldry should always follow an authentic design, appropriate to the period, and be shaped to fit the proportions of a man's head. Rivets, hinges, clasps, and the like may be shown for realism, but a well-drawn stylized version (like the esquire helmet below) is quite acceptable. The six helmets shown above are authentic examples of actual types.

The **salade** (above, left); early fourteenth century. Still earlier thirteenth century models were hat-like with a downward-slanting brim slotted for vision. Salades resembled inverted pots and slipped on over the head.

The **heaume** (second and third from left); fourteenth century; front and profile views of two similar styles. The weight of this helmet rested on the shoulders and was shaped to fit in place; unlike the salade, it could be fastened to the body armor. Basically a cylinder with truncated top, it was large and roomy, affording ample protection to head and neck. Round patterns of seven or nine holes often decorated both sides of the face. This style was commonly worn on the field of combat.

The great **tilting helms** were developed later; their vogue was in the fifteenth and sixteenth centuries and they became at that time favorites of heraldic artists. These helms were worn in tournaments and were designed for protection against the lance, thus the polished curves to turn the lance point and the heavy fastenings to secure them firmly to chest and shoulders. Visored helmets (below) are of a much later period.

Helmets and their positions came to serve a function in British heraldry they do not perform elsewhere. The monarch alone rates an open barred helmet of gold, displayed *affronté*. Knights are distinguished by an open-visored helmet, placed *affronté*. Esquires and gentlemen employ the closed tilting helm turned to dexter in profile. (The Scots reserve the tilting helm for barons and chiefs and the heaume for gentlemen.) All peers, including the monarch and the royal family, place a **chapeau** or **cap of maintenance** within their coronets. Members of royalty have special crowns; peers have **coronets** (as shown below right, with a chapeau beneath the coronet).

King   **Duke**   **Knight**   **Esquire**

When two sets of arms are impaled, the shield is bisected by a vertical line, the complete arms of the husband occupying the dexter half, the prenomial arms of the wife the sinister half. Borders on either arms are omitted down the dividing line of the shield.

The plain arms of Vice-Admiral Sir William Penn are shown next to those of William Penn of Pennsylvania bearing the cadency mark (p. 28) of a second son (during his father's lifetime). Below these are the impaled arms of William Penn III and his wife. To the right the plain arms of the wife are displayed on a lozenge, as are the arms of all ladies except a queen regnant. The impaled arms of a married couple would be transferred to a lozenge if the wife should become widowed.

Like quartering, the impaling of arms tends to diminish the visual importance of both arms. In an older form, arms were simply bisected and the two half-shields conjoined—which occasionally resulted in such amusing combinations as the forequarters of three leopards with the sterns of three ships.

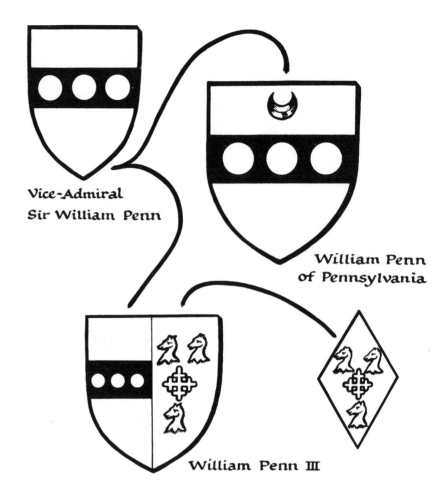

Vice-Admiral
Sir William Penn

William Penn
of Pennsylvania

William Penn III

Denmark Greece Mountbatten Edinburgh

Duke of Edinburgh

Prince Philip of England, Duke of Edinburgh, is a member of the royal family to which the present kings of Denmark, Greece, and Norway belong. With the royal arms of Denmark and Greece (his father's family), His Royal Highness quarters the arms of Mountbatten (his mother's family) and those of the royal city of Edinburgh, from which his title is derived.

When an arms contains simple quarters such as these, the combined effect is not unpleasant, although any one of the original simple shields is perhaps more powerful by itself. The Mountbatten shield is a particularly fine heraldic device.

ARMS OF
COCHRAN-PATRICK

Counter-Quartering

1- and 4 Counterquartered
   1-4 Patrick
   2-3 Cochran
2- Kennedy of Underwood
3- Hunter of Hunterston

ARMS OF
BROWN-WESTHEAD

Grand Quarterings

Quarterly:
1- Grand Quarter,
   Quarterly, Brown-Westhead
      1-4 Westhead
      2-3 Brown
2- Grand Quarter, Brown
3- Grand Quarter, Westhead
4- Grand Quarter, Chapell

ARMS OF
JERNINGHAM

Quarterly of Eight

Quarterly: *
1- Jerningham
2- Plowden
3- Howard
4- Thomas of Brotherton
5- Mowbray
6- Thomas of Woodstock:
      Quarterly: 1-4 France
                 2-3 England
7- Stafford
8- Bohun

Quartering, largely a British practice, is a method of combining in one shield the arms of two or more families. The Royal Arms of Great Britain (p. 30) is an example of simple quartering at its best, as is the shield of the Duke of Edinburgh on page 26. At its worst, quartering results in a patchwork of tinctures and charges that becomes a mere heraldic texture, negating its original purpose as an instantly recognizable mark of identification and becoming a sort of incomplete genealogy.

The mechanics of quartering are often complex. The arms of a man married to an armorial heiress (i.e., without brothers) is regularly impaled with hers. On her actual succession, however, he displays in the center of his own shield a small escutcheon bearing her arms — the *escutcheon* (or *shield*) *of pretense.* During their lifetime, the couple's children use only the paternal arms. Later the children will quarter their shields with the father's arms occupying the first and fourth quarters and the mother's the second and third.

Should the bearer of quartered arms marry an heiress, he impales his quartered arms with her simple achievement during the lifetime of her father; later he assumes an escutcheon of pretense. Ultimately his son will display in his third quarter the arms of his mother, replacing the arms of his grandmother, repeated from the second quarter. Should a fourth shield be introduced in the next generation, it is placed in the fourth quarter. Further quarters may be added as necessary, with the paternal quarter repeated last when the number of quarters is odd.

The greatest multiplicity of quartering occurs when an heiress' arms already has numerous quarters. The son may then display the quarters of both parents, those of his father coming first in numerical order. English shields may become quarterly of eight, as shown; quarterly of twenty; or, conceivably, quarterly of two hundred. For regular use, the quarterings may be reduced in number, but only according to very specific rules set by the College of Arms.

In Scotland, where quarters are held to four by the system of *Grand Quartering,* the quarters themselves are quartered — a method that is also used in some instances in England. The Scotch system arose from the fact that Scotch arms cannot be subdivided, the entire arms being counter-quartered, or carried intact as a quarter.

A woman who has brothers cannot ordinarily

transmit her arms to her children, since it is assumed that the arms will descend in the male line. All sisters in a family without sons, however, may transmit the family achievement. Should an heiress marry a man who does not have his own arms, the achievement of her family becomes extinct — her husband having no shield on which to display the arms of pretense. Nevertheless, by applying for a posthumous grant of her arms to her husband and his descendants, a rightful heir may regain the right to display these arms. (There are also special rules pertaining to adopted and natural children and to multiple marriages.)

The continued practice of multiple quartering has tended to diminish the artistic effect of the old simple shield. In principle, the shield should bear the insignia of one family only, because heraldry, with its roots in the entirely masculine activities of the battlefield and tournament ground, is based on the line of male descent. It is popularly believed that a many-quartered coat of arms is the mark of nobility or of the antiquity of a house; the British Royal Arms is ample proof to the contrary.

Escutcheon of Pretense

These marks have been used since the fourteenth century to indicate within a family the seniority of its different members by male descent.

A tincture not employed in the arms is recommended for cadency marks, and these marks are normally much smaller in proportion to the entire shield than drawn here.

Illustrated is the English sequence of marks of cadency. (A Scottish sequence is still in use, but it tends to become quite complicated, even for the professional herald, to say nothing of the descendants of long-lived Scotsmen.)

The *heir* or first son uses the **label**; the second son, the **crescent**; the third son, the **mullet**; the fourth son, the **martlet**; the fifth son, the **annulet**; the sixth son, the **fleur de lis**; the seventh son, the **rose**; the eighth son, the **cross moline**; and the ninth son, the **double quatrefoil** (not shown). Heraldry provides no cadency marks beyond the ninth son.

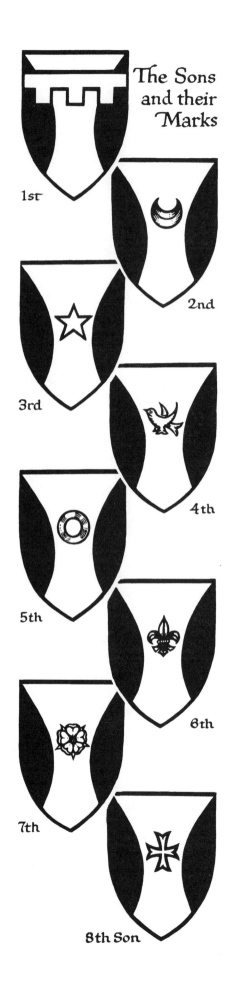

The Sons and their Marks

1st

2nd

3rd

4th

5th

6th

7th

8th Son

Washington

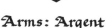
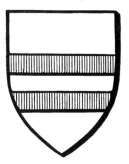

Arms: Argent   **2 bars Gules,**   **in chief 3 mullets of the 2nd**

Washington arms: Argent two bars and in chief three mullets gules.

Blazonry is the method of describing armorial bearings in a manner so precise and accurate that heraldic artists may render them exactly without the originals. Heraldic terminology is a colorful language derived largely from Old English and Old French. A blazon follows a regular sequence: First, the field is described and its tincture(s) named in order. If the field is divided, the type and character of division precedes the tinctures — per fess, argent and gules, for example, or per bend indented, azure and argent.

Next, the principal charge or charges are described and their characteristics and tinctures indicated.

Then, lesser charges on the field are described, followed by any lesser devices upon the principal charge or charges. Specification of border completes the description of the shield.

Description of the crest follows; after that the supporters, if any. Details of the mantling or the compartment (see p. 13) are not usually mentioned. The motto may be given or omitted.

Blazoning of quartered and multiquartered arms (see p. 27) is still common in British heraldry. Blazons of this type are highly complex but must be precise to be meaningful to the specialist.

When two arms are quartered simply upon one shield, quarters 1 and 4 (from dexter) are first blazoned, then 2 and 3. When the shield is quarterly of 6, 8, 10, 12, and so on, each numbered quartering is blazoned in turn from the dexter, the family name or national designation of each being explained with precision. (Quarterings of previously quartered Scottish arms must be blazoned intact in their turn. The technical knowledge needed to blazon a shield quarterly of 20, 25, 30, or more, is considerable. It is easy to understand why Scottish heralds who are held to the system of Grand Quarters [p. 27] find it prudent in many cases to drop the quarterings of intervening heiresses, retaining only those of true significance.) The remainder is blazoned in the usual manner.

A complete achievement, incidentally, may display more than one crest. This does not imply that the honorable gentleman involved has two or three heads, or that he collects those of relatives or ancestors; he merely affirms a right to all the crests that appear.

Tinctures, once they have been named for the field and principal device, are referred to when they recur as "of the first," "of the second," "of the third," based on the order in which they were introduced.

Bailey

Bailey arms: On a fess nebuly between four martlets, three in chief and one in base argent, two roses of the first (gules), barbed and seeded proper.

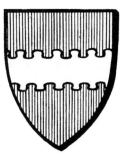

Arms: Gules, on a fess nebuly...   **between 4 martlets 3 in chief, 1 in base, Argent...**   **2 roses of the 1st barbed & seeded Proper.**

THE BRITISH ROYAL ARMS

The complete achievement of the Royal Family of Great Britain is illustrated and blazoned step by step for a clear understanding of how blazonry functions for more complex arms. The famous Plantagenet lions occupy quarters 1 and 4.

The second quarter contains the arms of Scotland and shows the famous Royal Tressure, "flory counter flory," referring to the *fleurs de lis* pointing alternately in and out of the border which encloses a lion rampant.

The third quarter always contains the Irish Harp, although it no longer represents all of the Emerald Isle. The golden harp with silver strings is representative of the North of Ireland and not Eire, which is now a republic. The harp and shamrock are Royal Irish Badges when displayed with the Royal Crown.

The royal arms is properly subject to certain changes when it happens to be displayed in Scotland. The arms of the Kingdom of Scotland is displayed on the first and fourth quarters, the English lions occupying the second quarter.

Arms~Quarterly~ 1st and 4th, Gules: 3 lions passant guardant in pale, Or, for England.

2nd~ Or, a lion rampant within

a double tressure flory counter flory, Gules: for Scotland.

3rd~ Azure, a harp Or, stringed Argent; for Ireland.

The Garter symbolizes the most notable Order of the Garter, established by Edward III in 1348. At a celebration following the capture of Calais, the King picked up a garter dropped by Joan, Countess of Salisbury. He gallantly wrapped the blue garter about his own left knee, rebuking jesting onlookers with the words *honi soit qui mal y pense,* "shamed be he who thinks evil of it." The blue garter was adopted as the badge of the Order, which consists of twenty-six knights, including the sovereign and leading peers.

The whole encircled with the Garter.

Crest~Upon the Royal helmet the Crown proper thereon a lion statant guardant, Or, crowned also proper.

"Armed, crined and unguled or" means that the unicorn's horn, mane, and hoofs are tinctured gold. *Dieu et mon droit* means "God and my right." Note that the crest opposes the position of the royal helm. In the Scotch version the lion is *affronté* and sitting erect, thus facing the same direction as the barred royal helmet.

Supporters ~On the dexter a lion guardant, Or, crowned as the crest; and on the sinister an unicorn Argent, armed, crined &

unguled Or and gorged with a coronet composed of crosses patee and fleurs de lis, a chain affixed thereto passing

between the forelegs and reflexed over the back of the last.

Motto "Dieu et mon droit"

Illustrated and emblazoned on this page is a collection of shields showing the ordinaries most commonly found in heraldry. The blazoning begins from the upper dexter angle of each shield and runs consecutively to the lower sinister (p. 17). The traditional system of hatching (p. 15) indicates the tincture of each part of the shield.

1. Per pale, sable and or.
2. Paly of four, argent and sable.
3. Argent, the dexter tierce gules.
4. Gules, a pale or.
5. Argent, a pallet (narrower than a pale) sable.
6. Per fesse, or and gules.
7. Barry of five, azure and argent.
8. Or, a chief azure.
9. Argent, a base gules. 10. Ermine, a base vert.
11. Or, a fesse gules. 12. Argent, a barrulet sable.
13. Per pale; the dexter half argent, the sinister half per fesse azure and or.
14. Per fesse; the upper half per pale sable and gules, the lower argent. 15. Quarterly, or and azure.
16. Checky of nine, vert and argent.
17. Checky of twenty, or and gules.
18. Quarterly: the 1st and 4th per pale, argent and gules; the 2nd and 3rd or.
19. Per fesse, gules and argent, a pale counterchanged.
20. Per pale, barry of five, or and azure, counterchanged.
21. Paly of six, argent and sable, a fesse counterchanged.
22. Or, a cross gules.
23. Argent, a dexter canton sable.
24. Azure, a chief point ermine.
25. Per bend, or and vert.
26. Per bend sinister, argent and azure.
27. Or; in the dexter chief a triangle sable.
28. Barruly, vert and argent. 29. Or, a bend gules.
30. Bendy sinister of six, azure and argent.
31. Per saltire, vert and argent.
32. Per bend, the dexter half argent, the sinister per bend sinister, vert and or.
33. Per bend sinister, bendy of six, sable and argent, counterchanged.
34. Lozengy, argent and azure.
35. Fusilly, argent and azure. 36. Or, a pile azure.
37. Azure, a pile argent, issuing from the sinister side.
38. Gyronny of four, argent and gules, issuing from the dexter chief point.
39. Or, a chevron vert.
40. Chevronny of six, azure and argent.
41. Party per pale and saltire, gules and argent.
42. Gyronny of eight, or and azure.
43. Argent, a gyron azure, moving from the dexter side. 44. Per pall, sable, argent and gules.
45. Per pall, reversed, or, argent and azure.
46. Argent, a pall gules.
47. Pily barwise, argent and azure.
48. Per fesse angled, argent and gules.

49. Per fesse escartely, azure and or.
50. Or, a pile indented sable, also per chevron indented, or and sable.
51. Per bend indented, azure and argent.
52. Per pale potented, argent and azure.
53. Per fesse potented, or and gules.
54. Per fesse dentilly, gules and argent.
55. Per fesse nebuly, azure and argent.
56. Sable, a chief engrailed, or, also per fesse engrailed, or and sable.
57. Argent, a pale raguly. 58. Or, a bend indented.
59. Argent, a bend sinister wavy azure.
60. Azure, a cross engrailed or.

LYONS   FORREST   WOLFE   SMITH   A FARMER   AN ACTOR

Most Americans who are entitled to family arms and who are interested in displaying them generally know what those arms are. Those people who are interested in finding out whether or not they may legitimately use an existing coat of arms can find the answer, although the investment of time, energy, and some money will be involved. Genealogy may be verified by consulting standard works on the subject (beginning perhaps with information in the family Bible); there are a number of reputable professional experts who will do the necessary research; and the heraldic authorities of the family's country of origin can furnish information. Generally speaking, only those who can actually show direct lineage through the male line are legitimately authorized to claim specific existing arms.

There is in almost everyone at one time or another the desire to recapture the pageantry and color of the distant past of an age — such as the Age of Chivalry — that seems to us heroic, and for many people this arouses the desire to find an ancestral link with that past.

A universal human desire — and one that is both stronger and more individual than an occasional nostalgia for the real or fancied romance of earlier centuries — is that for a strong and unique identity; this can be expressed by adopting a personal symbol or particular combination of symbols. In fact, this is one of the strong sources of modern heraldry as we know it: the knight indeed needed and wanted an insigne that was instantly recognizable on the battlefield, a sign to which he could rally his forces; he also wanted a symbol that was uniquely associated with his name, whether on the jousting ground or his personal banner or on the façade of his manor house, to be passed on to his heir.

Our society today, nurtured on the changing centuries since knighthood came to full flower and infused particularly with the spirit of the New World, has abandoned the rigid and prescribed class structure of the Western world during the late Middle Ages and the Renaissance. There is today a new and often justifiable pride in the consciousness of personal en-

deavor and individual accomplishment. So today, although the possessor of time-honored armorial bearings can and often does display them with pride, many feel that it is perfectly sensible to create an entirely new emblem symbolic of a man's real personal accomplishment (honestly and simply using bona fide heraldic methods) rather than unimaginatively to copy, adapt, or appropriate somebody else's arms simply because they have been in existence longer. The new design becomes a valid personal symbol; in so establishing new arms, the bearer is establishing an heirloom instead of continuing one.

Examples of possible new arms are shown at the top of page 33 and the foot of page 34. Newly established family arms can be designed in the long tradition of punning on the family name, or they can be indicative of a profession. Such arms can be used in bookplates, on stationery, on flags, in architectural decoration, and in other ways — as personal arms have been used through the centuries.

The most important step in developing a coat of arms is to decide on the character of the shield — its shape, divisions, charges and their placement and the tinctures that will show them off to the best advantage.

The shape of the shield is entirely arbitrary, a question of individual taste. Of the so-called heraldic forms, the heater and the tilting shield are the most popular and the easiest to work with. The round, oblong, and almond shapes were used for many centuries and cannot honestly be ignored. But, heraldically speaking, the first two are the best choice. The later Baroque and strapwork shields require careful matching of period styling in helmet, mantling, and crest elements, and a technique of rendering that is compatible with their periods, with no assurance for the novice of an authentic creation, since the available models are both notoriously unreliable and poorly contrived. Having chosen the shape of the shield, the designer must now create the arms to be displayed upon it.

The face of the shield may be composed in several ways. It may consist of a plain field, a field with an ordinary, or with an ordinary and other charges, or a semé of charges, or any combination of these that is heraldically correct.

The colors of heraldry (see p. 15) in modern English are: red, blue, green, tan, purple and black, with the yellow of gold and the white of silver. Imitations of the two common furs, ermine and vair, also appear: ermine, white with black tails; vair, shown with alternating patches of blue and white. The simple heraldic rule that metal must not be placed upon metal nor color upon color arose logically from the necessity for clear and quick identification by ensuring the best possible contrast. In designing a new coat of arms, use light colors upon dark and dark against light. Gold, for example, shows up better on a deep blue than a pale azure.

The field may be of any one tincture, by itself — any metal, color, or fur. Or it may be of any two tinctures — two metals, two colors or furs, since these are placed next to one another, not upon one another. Or the combination may be of metal and color, metal and fur, or color and fur. All tinctures are of equal heraldic rank and have no special significance in armory, and any shade or value is permissable.

On the field, two tinctures are arranged per pale, per fess, per bend, per chevron, cross or saltire. (Study p. 17, then p. 32.) When three tinctures are used upon a field, it is "tierced," as tierced in fess, bend, pale, etc. In all these cases, the lines of division follow the direction of the ordinary indicated.

Having decided the tincturing of the field, its division (if any), and the possible use of one or more ordinaries, we may now impose the various objects known as charges upon any or all of its component parts. A single charge may be imposed upon a shield, but groups of two, three, or four are common, with three the most frequent grouping. Charges must follow the general rule of tinctures and should fill comfortably the spaces they occupy. In modern heraldry, when charges are referred to as *proper,* they often appear in true natural colors, with the possibility of poor visual effect. In older heraldry, the term meant to tincture as closely as possible to nature using the heraldic tinctures — *not the colors of nature.*

The vigorous and striking charges of beasts and birds that graced the shields of knights and nobles in early heraldry are seldom surpassed today for visual sophistication and style. The ability to distinguish these large, uncluttered, and well-balanced forms from a distance was the heraldic ideal of the old days. The tradition of painting charges in solid flat silhouette without shading or modeling is still worth careful consideration.

Blazonry (see p. 29) is a method of describing armorial bearings in a precise and accurate manner so that heraldic artists may render them without having seen the originals. It may also offer to the novice a step-by-step method of designing a heraldic device. Proceed as the blazon proceeds, building your design as the blazon does and there is little chance of failure. Use the shields on page 32 with their blazons as a beginning, and practice building upon them. (See examples of new arms at the top of p. 33 and the foot of p. 34.)

There are a few precautions to be observed in designing a coat of arms. Avoid quartering the shield

PROFESSOR

PUBLISHER

OIL PRODUCER

and filling each quarter with entirely unrelated gimmicks or emblems. Avoid ridiculous quarterings reminiscent of royalty or nobility. Avoid supporters and the helmets and mantlings reserved for peers. When developing a modern coat of arms, such affectations are presumptuous and neither original nor meaningful. Also avoid the use of letters or numerals on the shield. They destroy its dignity and uniqueness. This last is the most common failing of commercial devices.

Since heraldry has been in existence since about A.D. 1150, it is only to be expected that most of the inevitable combinations of charges and ordinaries have long since been utilized by armorial families of the past. Despite this situation, heralds have little difficulty in establishing a recognizable difference between similar shields. Duplication is avoided by the expedient of inventing or employing a charge or charges never before used. The designer can find fresh material in many places. For example, the Oriental and Semitic cultures provide a wealth of symbols that were rarely, if ever, used in earlier armory.

It is possible to compile an almost endless list of "American" charges that, simply drawn and stylized in the heraldic manner, can produce new and valid coats of arms. The New World abounds in wildlife not to be found elsewhere: the moose, the turkey, the bison, the rattlesnake, the native eagles and hawks, owls, songsters, and aquatic birds. To these may be added Indian symbols, tools and weapons, Amish or Pennsylvania Dutch designs, cattle-brands and historic objects. Arms that employ such charges will be different, assertive and frankly original.

Once the shield design has been perfected, you may select a helmet to go with it, a crest, torse and mantling, and finally, a motto. Either the heaume or tilting helmet is considered a good choice. They may face affronté or be turned partially or fully to dexter profile. Helmet position has no meaning in this country. However, in Great Britain, it still denotes rank. Unless you wish to indicate knighthood or a title, avoid using either an open-visored or barred helmet.

Your crest emblem can be borrowed from your shield (see Scandinavian and Teutonic arms). It should face the same direction as the helmet — for example — a rampant lion, normally dexter, requires a helmet turned dexter profile. Examples in this book that violate this rule were reproduced as we found them and serve to underline the absurd practice of having the crest face in a direction differing from that of the helmet.

The mantling usually takes its colors from the principal metal and color of the shield.

With regard to commercial or trade devices, certain questions must be carefully considered. What is the intent and purpose of the design and has it been accomplished? On what backgrounds will it be reproduced? Is the linework and rendering strong enough for both reduction and enlargement? Will it print well in reverse? Is it easy to recognize and remember? Does it resemble any competing device too closely? Does it tie in dramatically with the organization or product involved? Is the dignity of the shield unsullied by lettering, initials, or numerals? Does it honor the rules of heraldry? And . . . is it beautiful?

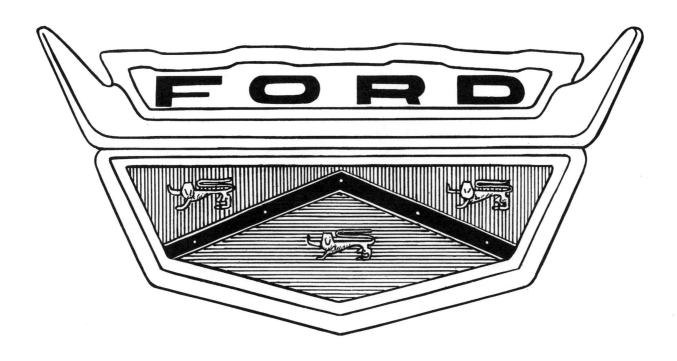

Calligraphy means "beautiful writing." Although modern typography has developed a profusion of styles, the examples on these two pages show basic hand-drawn styles. It is important to apply a suitable calligraphy to any heraldic design.

Calligraphy should be visually pleasing, free, and well spaced. Space the letters by eye — never measure. Watch letter proportion and proper placement of cross bars and serifs. Leave width of an *m* between words.

ABCDEFGHIJ
KLMNOPQR
STUVWXYZ
ISE *write plain capitals minus serifs; then, using small pen or brush draw serifs so they appear to 'grow' gracefully out of the letters.*

SQUARE ROMAN CAPS →
Pen Angle 30° ABO

ABCDEFGHIJKLMN
OPQRSTUVWXYZ-J

ABCDEFGHIJKLMN
OPQRSTUVWXYZ-J

← Built-up Capitals
IFO *Do inside first-add weight outside.* (Note)
Use small pen-hold it Flat on strokes. *Uprights curve inward.*

Practice this simple Roman first, using a flat, chiseled pen of the Speedball "C" series, a manuscript text-writing nib with reservoir, a lettering brush, or a chiseled pencil. Strokes form the letters as shown, but overlap them without showing joinings. Nib angle 30 degrees. The Classic Roman at right may be designed upon these basic forms.

Square Roman capitals have written rather than designed serifs. Hold the 30-degree nib angle throughout the entire letter, including the serifs. These forms are quickly written, have a formal dignity and great legibility. They are always appropriate devices because of their Latin origin.

The built-up capitals are first sketched, then built up with a smaller square-edged pen. A stub nib is suitable, although some calligraphers prefer a brush. Colored inks and pen produce a weak effect; use a brush in brilliant tempera when color is called for.

The Old English and other black-letter styles are written with the chisel of the pen at a 45-degree angle. Capitals are never used together. This style is a favorite in church heraldry, municipal arms and citations.

ABCDEFGHIJKLMN
OPQRSTUVWXYZ✛
abcdefghijklmnopqrstuvwxyz

← Old English
45°
Spurs
Serifs
Pointed pen for hairlines
nosh

Flemish	1100
Rotunda	1300
Fractur	1400
Batarde	1400

A B C D E F G H I J K L M N
O P Q R S T U V W X Y Z & &

abcdefghijklmnopqrstuvwxyz

Edge of pen held at 45° angle to line of writing *45°*
Capital height, 8 pen widths **AB** *Small letters 5 widths of pen in height* *abgi*
✳ *Ascenders 5 pen widths above; descenders 5 below*

Chancery Cursive employs sloping Roman capitals with decorative swashes; the lower-case letters are written compactly, touching at times but never letter-spaced. Follow the pen scale and writing rules closely; this form requires practice to master.

GOTHIC OR FUTURA

**ABCDEFGHI
JKLMNOPQ
RSTUVWXYZ
abcdefghijklm
nopqrstuvwxyz**

'Speedball' Method: For finer finish
'Square Off' — Or rule-out with pen and compass — compass curves

Sans-serif lettering is not calligraphic, being based on the printing type called Futura. On curved motto scrolls it may be imitated by stroking in with a "B" series Speedball, then squaring off with a ruling pen. White tempera can be used with a small brush to touch up. This may be rendered nicely with ruling pen and compass, much larger than final size, then reduced by photostat for sharpness. All strokes are of even thickness.

Hold pen flat: abcdefghijklm nopqrstuvwxyz

Irish Uncial is a rounded style that has seldom been used since the tenth century except for decorative purposes. Hold the pen with the nib on a plane horizontal to the line of writing.

A B C D E F G H I J K L M N O
P Q R S T U V W X Y Z &

abcdefghijklmnopqrstuvwxyz &

Humanist Bookhand uses freely written square Roman capitals; the small letters are the basis for all book types. They use simple hooked serifs or sharp beaks formed with an additional touch of the pen.

*A B C D E F G H I J K L M
N O P Q R S T U V W X Y Z*
abcdefghijklmnopqrstuvwxyz

Build-up Roundhand, rule straights–draw in curves freely–Note curves are truly round *60°* *use guides* *Correct* *Draw* *Wrong*

Roundhand, the favorite of old writing masters, was originally written with a quill; now it is rendered with a flexible steel pen. Pressure on the downstroke produces the thickness. Build it up much larger than desired for final use, then reduce for sharpness.

*A B C D E F G H I J K L M
N O P Q R S T U V W X Y Z*

Lombardic is obtainable from typesetters. These built-up uncials resemble the built-up capitals and are designed in the same manner. A brush may prove superior to a pen on this form.

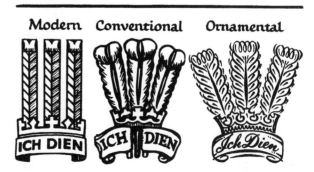

Modern   Conventional   Ornamental
ICH DIEN   ICH DIEN   Ich Dien

Style versus style. The three examples shown here of the crest of the Prince of Wales illustrate how a style of lettering can complement a style of execution. Harmony between the parts of a design is a safe course.

HALLMARK OF QUALITY

GARRARD

Furniture by
DINOLEVI

GOHRSMÜHLE

WINSOR & NEWTON LTD
LONDON

John Hancock
LIFE INSURANCE COMPANY
OF BOSTON, MASSACHUSETTS

Western Auto

Le plus grand nom du COGNAC

SACER PACIS CUSTOS

PRINCE de
POLIGNAC

SERMONA CONSONA FACTA

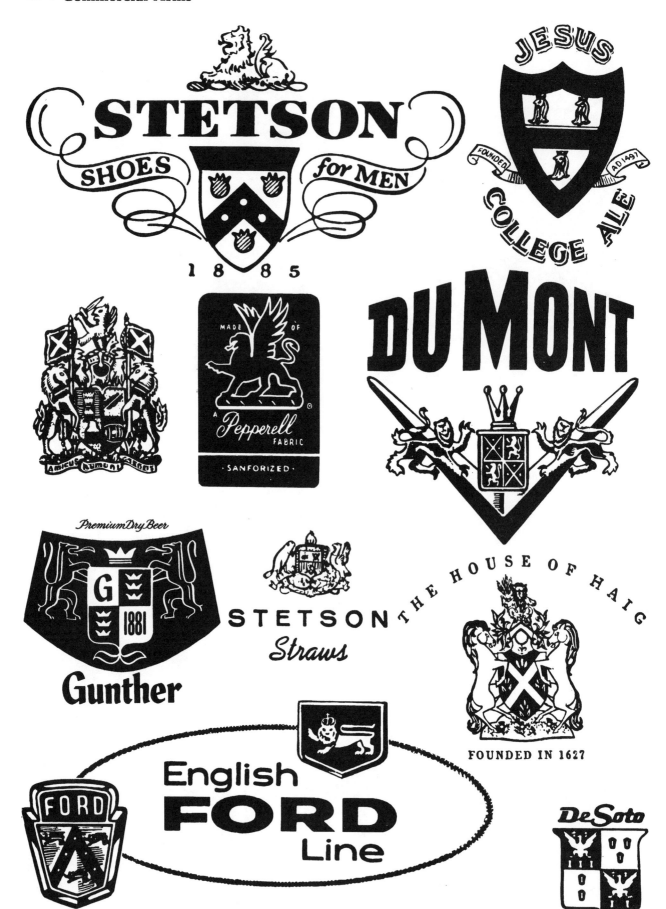

ARMS OF THE WORLD

The arms illustrated on pp. 44–73 have been chosen as examples of typical arms and for the quality of their design. They will be of interest both to the artist and to the general reader, but they should not be used as the only basis for detailed large-scale copying, nor should they be considered other than a representative sampling of the many coats of arms in existence.

BARTLETT

PECK

GREER

WALLER

SPOTTISWOODE

LOVEJOY

WRIGHT

HORD

RANKIN

SWIFT

HERRICK

SULLIVAN

MOSELEY

O'HANLY

VAUGHAN

BANCROFT

BOONE

NEWINGTON

BALL

TOWER

JONES

WEST

WALDEN

CROSBY

ROBERTSON

SYMINGTON

COIT

WASHINGTON

BOYD

HASELL

BAGBY

STEVENS

BIRCH

RICE

HINNISDAL

DENBY

VEITCH

NICHOLS

MORTON

STOKES

GORIANSKY

WOOLLEY

ROBERTSON

URQUHART

ABELL

BROCK

BUTLER

BANKES

JONES

HUME

ESTCOURT

LEE

BURGOYNE-WALLACE

HOLBECH

ERSKINE

BARTELOT

ADAMS

BLADON

CADELL

BLAGG

LECHMERE

LLOYD

BIRRELL

BAILEY

BUTCHER

ALLIX

BROCK

HEADLUM

PHINEASBURY

BUTLER

BARCLAY

COMBE

ALLISON

LLOYD

PETER-HOBLYN

GATAKER

ELMHIRST

DARROCH

FANSHAWE

SPENCE-COLBY

GRIFFITH

D'ARCY

BATCHELOR

CADDY

LOVEDAY

BOULTON

BAILLIE

DAVIES

CLARK

BASTARD

JONES

PRO·PATRIA·ET·REGE

BAKER

LOVE·AND·DREAD

HOBHOUSE

MELIORA SPERO

FULLERTON

LUX·IN·TENEBRIS

HOHLER

DEUM·TIMEO

LLOYD

COKER

FIAT·JUSTITIA

CORBET

DEUS·PASCIT·CORVOS

BERIDGE

McNAIR

GARDINER

ROBERTSON

SHUCKFORTH

TRIBLE

JEFFERYS

GADSDEN

SUNDERLAND

READ

CAMPBELL

ASKEW

McGUFFIE

COX

CRAUFURD

BIRKMYRE

MACKINTOSH

DRUMMOND

FARQUHARSON

FARIE

SHAW-MACKENZIE

CAMPBELL

HAMILTON

McDOUALL

FINLAY

MACDUFF

GUTHRIE

MEIKLE

JOHNSTON

INNES

HOUSTON

McEWEN

GORDON

SCOTT-McKIRDY

McGRIGOR

CAMPBELL

GORDON

HENNESSY

O'CONOR

MAHON

MaCCARTIE

MORONY

WALSH

BOYLE

CARROLL

TIGHE

PRESTON

ROE

KAVANAGH

DAY

MOORE

GRAHAM

O'CONNOR-MORRIS

CONOLLY

VAUGHAN

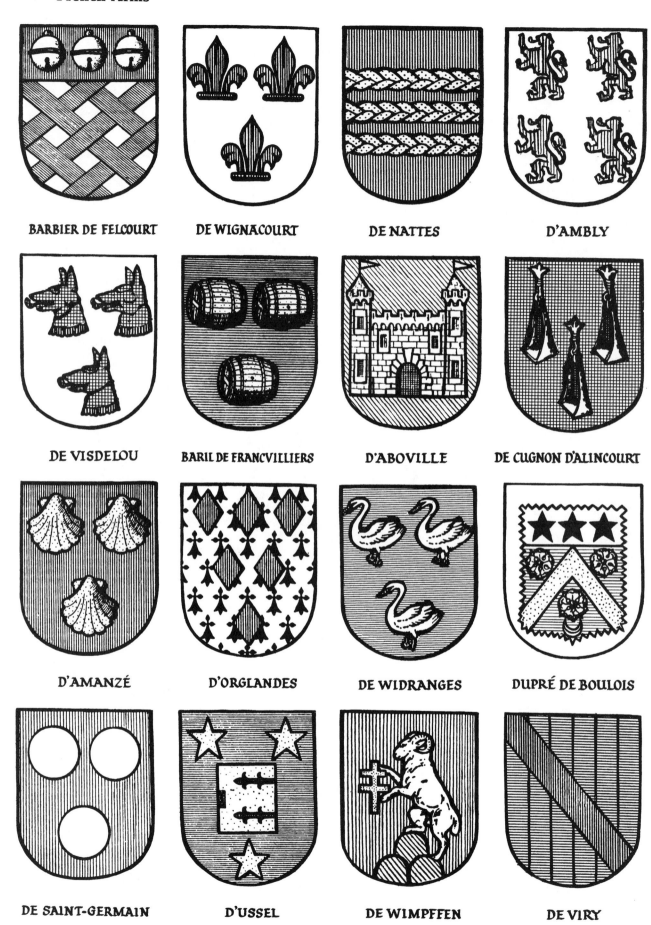

BARBIER DE FELCOURT   DE WIGNACOURT   DE NATTES   D'AMBLY

DE VISDELOU   BARIL DE FRANCVILLIERS   D'ABOVILLE   DE CUGNON D'ALINCOURT

D'AMANZÉ   D'ORGLANDES   DE WIDRANGES   DUPRÉ DE BOULOIS

DE SAINT-GERMAIN   D'USSEL   DE WIMPFFEN   DE VIRY

DES ROTOURS   DE SAINT-GILLES   DE POMPERY   D'ESCONDÉCA DE BOISSE

DE MAUPEOU   D'ABON   DE ROTON   CORRET

TESTU DE BALINCOURT   DE WALSH   D'ERARD   DE RIVIÈRE

DE WATTEVILLE   DE WAVRECHIN   DUPRÉ DE SAINT-MAUR   D'ASTORG

GAMA

AYMERICH

ANDRADE

VARGAS

TENORIO

MAGALLÓN

BESORA

ENVEIG

ELÍO

CASTELLBÓ

MAZA

TRILLO

CARRILLO

VILLALOBOS

OSSONA

LUNA

ZAFORTEZA   BETHENCOURT   TARRAGONA   CLEMENTE

ESPEJO   VALLSECA   BRAGANZA   CRESPI

CASTRO   BALBOA   OLID   GARRO

COPONS   CRUILLES   OVIEDO   ILLA

ALBANI   BADOER   BALDINOTTI   ADORNO

BALDINI   BALBI   BALBIANO   ALBERGHETTI

ACCIARDI   BARATELLI   ANTONELLI   BALSANO

ABBATI MARESCOTTI   ANTONELLI   AMICO~PATERNO   AGNINI

ADAMI

AGOSTI

AMICO

BARNI

ABBONDI

ABRO D'PAGRATIDE

BALSAMO

BARACCA

ADAMO

ACERBO

BAIARDI

BAGATTI-VALSECCHI

ABBATE

ANTONELLI

ADDA ᔕ SALVATERRA

BAROFFIO DALL'AGLIO

VOIGT

HAACK

ECKERT

RAPS

HILL

AMEIS

SCHULTZE

PFIEFFER

BECK

BUCKHOLTZ

ERNST

HAUSCHILDT

CONSTANTIN

BOEGLE

WINTER

GLÜCK

MARSCHALL

VOGEL

LINDGREN

HILDEBRAND

SCHERLAG

ADENSTAM

RUNQUIST

BOHEMAN

NYSTRÖMER

WIJKSTRÖM

ARENANDER

LUNDQUIST

ROSENGREN

KOCH

HOLMSTEDT

HASSELROT

PEHRSSON-BRAMSTORP

BURÉN

SJÖGREN

SCHLYTER

SAMSONOFF

RAIEVSKY

KORYBUT-DACHKEVITCH

DERFELDEN

BYSTREEVSKY

TCHAPLINE

BAJENOFF

RYNDINE

KLOBOUKOFF

ROGOVITCH

LEVITZKY

ASTAKHOFF

DRENTELN

ZAREMBA

SOKOLOVSKY

BEKORIOUKOFF

YOURENEFF

DEMIANOFF

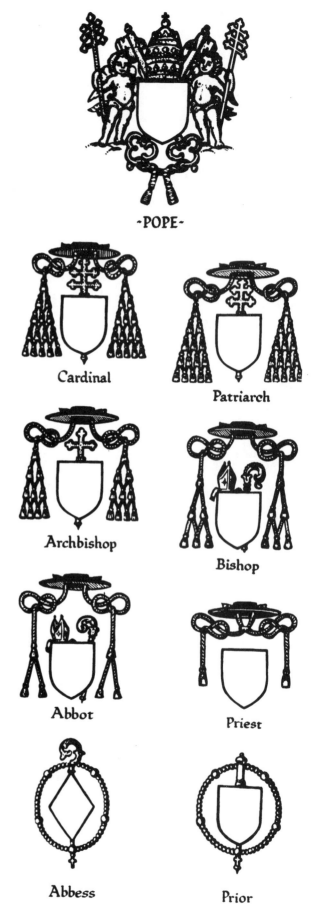

-POPE-

Cardinal

Patriarch

Archbishop

Bishop

Abbot

Priest

Abbess

Prior

The arms of the Pope are usually displayed with his **papal timbre** (or **timber**); the great triple tiara is placed above the shield with the keys of St. Peter — a gold key in bend dexter across a silver one in sinister — behind the shield. The present form has been in use with only minor change since about the middle of the sixteenth century.

Members of the clergy ranking below the Pope have symbols of their own which clearly indicate their offices. The cardinal's hat is red with red tassels; all other clergy have green hats and tassels except the priest, whose hat and tassels are black. Patriarchs and archbishops weave gold through their tassels; bishops, abbots, and priests do not. The cardinal displays fifteen red tassels on either side; the patriarch fifteen green tassels; the archbishop ten green tassels; the bishop six green tassels; the abbot three. The priest has one tassel on either side. The gold crosses of cardinals and patriarchs have two bars, an archbishop's has one. The crozier of a bishop curls to sinister, that of abbot and abbess to dexter; the prior has a pilgrim's staff. The abbess encircles her lozenge with a rosary, the prior does the same with his shield. Papal arms, displayed without the great tiara and crossed keys of St. Peter, are for the most part typical

LEO IX
1049~1054

GREGORY X
1271 ~ 1276

LEO XIII
1878~1903

URBAN V
1362~1370

INNOCENT IV
1243~1254

heraldic devices common to many of the noble and ancient families of Europe, most of whom have borne characteristically simple shields since early days.

A few popes have chosen to abandon the arms of their families for new devices of their own creation, possibly as an expression of humility or the desire to avoid profiting from the prestige of their families' rank.

Although heraldry shows little proof of existing before A.D. 1150, there are many examples of armorial bearings of popes who lived a full century before this date. These were beyond doubt created when, after 1580, there appeared a number of volumes dealing with the lives of the popes of preceding centuries. Most of these were illustrated with portraits, largely imaginary, of earlier popes — with small coats of arms in the background. These volumes, published independently of the church in various countries, seem to have been the source for most papal arms up to around 1200. Eventually papal and church heraldry passed through the Baroque and Rococo periods, as did secular heraldry, with characteristic changes in shield shapes and the addition of decorative elements. Cherubs, angels, saints, and other figures appeared as decorative supporters well into the 1900s.

URBAN III
1185~1187

HADRIAN IV
1154~1159

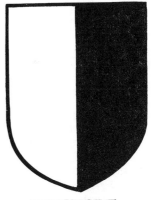

BENEDICT II
1303~1304

EUGENIUS
1431~1447

ALEXANDER II
1061~1073

PIUS III
1503~1503

MARTIN V
1417~1431

UNITED STATES OF AMERICA

ARGENTINA

BOLIVIA

BRAZIL

CHILE

Seal of the Treasury

PARAGUAY

COSTA RICA

CUBA

DOMINICAN REPUBLIC

ECUADOR

EL SALVADOR

HAITI

HONDURAS

MEXICO

NICARAGUA

PANAMA

GUATEMALA

PERU

COLOMBIA

URUGUAY

VENEZUELA

THE KINGS COUNCIL, COLONY OF VIRGINIA—1606

NEW PLYMOUTH COLONY—1620

NEW NETHERLANDS—1623

MASSACHUSETTS COLONY—1628

PETER STUYVESANT
GOVERNOR OF NEW AMSTERDAM—1642

VIRGINIA COLONY AFTER RESTORATION—1652

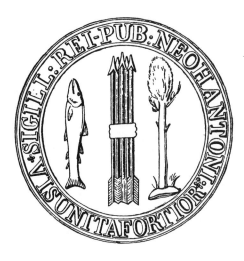

NEW HAMPSHIRE COLONY—1680

WILLIAM PENN, GOVERNOR AND PROPRIETOR
OF PENNSYLVANIA—1682

THE OHIO COMPANY—1749

JOHN MURRAY, EARL OF DUNMORE
GOVERNOR OF VIRGINIA—1772

CHRISTOPHER COLUMBUS' COAT
OF ARMS WHEN HE WAS MADE
DUKE OF VERAGUA

THE PRESIDENT

THE SENATE

THE HOUSE OF REPRESENTATIVES

THE SUPREME COURT

DEPT. OF STATE

DEPT. OF AIR FORCE

WAR OFFICE

DEPT. OF COMMERCE

DEPT. OF DEFENSE

DEPT. OF INTERIOR

DEPT. OF JUSTICE

DEPT. OF LABOR

NAVY DEPT.

POST OFFICE DEPT.

DEPT. OF AGRICULTURE

DEPT. OF INTERIOR

UNITED STATES OF AMERICA

ALABAMA

ALASKA

ARIZONA

ARKANSAS

CALIFORNIA

COLORADO

CONNECTICUT

DELAWARE

FLORIDA

GEORGIA

HAWAII

IDAHO

ILLINOIS

INDIANA

IOWA

KANSAS

KENTUCKY

LOUISIANA

MAINE

MARYLAND

MASSACHUSETTS

MICHIGAN

MINNESOTA

MISSISSIPPI

MISSOURI

MONTANA

NEBRASKA

NEVADA

NEW HAMPSHIRE

NEW JERSEY

NEW MEXICO

NEW YORK

NORTH CAROLINA

NORTH DAKOTA

OHIO

OKLAHOMA

OREGON

PENNSYLVANIA

RHODE ISLAND

SOUTH CAROLINA

SOUTH DAKOTA

TENNESSEE

TEXAS

UTAH

VERMONT

VIRGINIA

WASHINGTON

WEST VIRGINIA

WISCONSIN

WYOMING

WASHINGTON D.C.

PUERTO RICO

CANAL ZONE, ISTHMUS OF PANAMA

VIRGIN ISLANDS

JOHNS HOPKINS

NOTRE DAME

The readings offered below are a selective list that may prove of special interest to readers of this volume who would like to pursue additional studies in the field.

BIBLIOGRAPHY

Arnold, Oren. *Hot Irons*. Heraldry of the range. New York, Macmillan, 1940.

Bergling, John Mauritz. *Heraldic Designs and Engravings for the Workshop, Studio and Library*. Chicago, J. M. Bergling, c.1913.

Bodwitch, Harold. *Early Water Color Paintings of New England Coats of Arms*. Colonial Society of Massachusetts. Boston. v. 35, 1951. pp. 172-210.

Boutell's *Heraldry*. Rev. by C. W. Scott-Giles. London, Frederick Warne, 1958.

Burke, Sir Bernard. *The General Armory of England, Scotland, Ireland and Wales*. London, Burke's Peerage, 1961.

Cobb, Gerald. *The Colour of Heraldry*. Text by H. B. Pereira, M. Maclagan and C. R. Humphery-Smith. London, The Heraldry Society, 1958.

de Lannoy, Mortimer Delano. *The Heraldic Assembly of America, 1492-1905*. New York, 1905.

Eve, George W. *Heraldry as Art*. New York, Scribner's, 1907.

Franklyn Julian. *Shield & Crest*. Fwd. by A. C. T. White. Illus. by Norman Mainwaring. New York, Sterling, 1960.

Galbreath, Donald Lindsey. *Manuel du Blason*. Lausanne, Spes, rev. 1942.

Hope, W. H. St. John. *A Grammar of English Heraldry*. Cambridge University Press, 1913, rev. by Anthony Wagner, 1953.

————. *Heraldry for Craftsmen and Designers*. New York, Macmillan, 1913. Knowles, Charles. *Bolton's American Armory*. Boston, Faxon, 1927.

Koch, Rudolph. *The Book of Signs*. Trans. by Vyvyan Holland. New York, Dover, 1930.

Lancour, Harold. *Heraldry*. New York Public Library Bulletin, 1938.

Lehner, Ernst. *The Picture Book of Symbols*. New York, Wm. Penn, 1956.

London, H. Stanford. *The Right Road for the Study of Heraldry*. East Knoyle, Wiltshire, Heraldry Society, rev. by C. R. Humphrey-Smith, 1960.

Mladen, Leo M. *Arms and Names: Bartolus on the Right to Bear Arms*. Recueil du 5. Congrès International des Sciences Généalogique et Héraldique, Stockholm, 1961.

Moncreiffe, Iain and Don Pottinger. *Simple Heraldry*. New York, Thomas Nelson, 1953.

Papworth's *Ordinary of British Armorials*. Intro. by G. D. Squibb and R. Wagner. London, Tabard Publications, 1961.

Parker, J. H. *A Glossary of Terms Used in British Heraldry*. London, James Parker, 1894.

Reynolds, E. E. *Introduction to Heraldry*. London, Methuen, 1951.

Reynolds, J. A. *Heraldry and You*. New York, Thomas Nelson, 1961.

Rietstap, J. B. *Armorial Général*. Gouda, van Goor, 2nd ed., 1884-1887, 2 v.

Rolland, V. *Planches de l'Armorial Général de J. B. Rietstap*. v. 1-4 Paris, Institut héraldique, 1903-1912; v. 5-6, La Haye, Nijhoff, 1921-1926.

Ruggles, Henry Stoddard. *The "Herald Painters" of New England of the 18th and Early 19th Centuries*. Wakefield, Mass. 1924.

Shafter, Edmund Farwell. *Royal Arms and Other Regal Emblems and Memorials in Use in the Colonies Before the American Revolution*. (paper) Delivered before the Massachusetts Historical Society. Privately printed, Boston, 1889.

Stephanson, Jean. *Heraldry for the American Genealogist*. Drawings by Azalea Green Badgley. Washington, D. C., National Genealogical Society, 1959.

Valcourt-Vermont, Edgar de. *America Heraldica*. New York, Brentano Bros., 1886.

Wagner, Anthony. *Heraldry in England*. Harmondsworth, Penguin, 1946.

————. *Heralds and Heraldry in the Middle Ages*. Oxford University Press, 2nd ed., 1956.

————. *Historic Heraldry of Britain*. Oxford University Press, 1939.

Whittick, Arnold. *Symbols, Signs and Their Meaning*. Newton, Mass., Charles T. Bradford. 1960.

GLOSSARY—INDEX

NOTE: All terms are defined in their heraldic context only.

ABATEMENT; *see also* Augmentation
  Any figure added to a coat of arms which lowers the station of the bearer.

ACCOSTED
  Side by side.

ACHIEVEMENT, 12
  Full armorial honors.

ADDORSED, 18
  Turned back to back.

AFFRONTÉ, 19, 24
  Facing the viewer.

ALLERION
  Eagle displayed, without beak or feet.

American arms, 44–48

American flag, 22

American republics, arms of, 76–77

Animals, heraldic, 18–20

ANNULET, 17, 27
  A small circular charge, shaped like a ring; cadency mark for a fifth son.

ANTELOPE, 18
  Has the body of a stag, tail of a lion, two straight horns, and a short tusk on its nose.

APPAUMÉ, 24
  Palm of hand toward viewer.

ARGENT, 15
  Silver.

ARM, HUMAN, 24
  As a charge, shown couped at shoulder and bent with hand turned dexter (*embowed*) or sinister (*counterembowed*).

ARMED
  Animal or bird shown with its natural weapons of defense tinctured differently than the rest of its body.

ASSURGENT
  Man or beast rising from the sea.

AT GAZE, 18
  Stag standing, shown full-face.

AT SPEED
  Stag running.

AUGMENTATION, 16; *see also* Abatement
  An addition to existing arms granted as a reward or honor.

AVERSANT
  Showing the back.

AZURE, 15
  Blue.

BADGE
  Distinctive mark worn by those beneath the rank of gentleman, who therefore have no right to armorial bearings.

Bailey arms, 29

BANNER
  A square piece of silk or other cloth, attached to a pole or staff, bearing a heraldic device.

BAR, 16
  An ordinary occupying one fifth of the field, formed by two horizontal lines placed anywhere in the field.

BARBED, 21, 27

BARRULET
  Smallest diminutive of the bar, one fourth its size.

BARRY, 16
  Diminutive of bar; a *barry of six* is a shield divided into six bars.

BASE, 16
  Lower part of the field; any figure placed in the lower part of the shield is said to be *in base*.

BASILISK
  A monster similar to the wivern, but with a dragon's head at the end of his tail.

BATON
  Diminutive of the bend, one eighth its width; does not extend to the edges of the shield.

Bear, 18

Beasts, 18–19

Bee, 20

BELLED, 20, 24
  With bells affixed.

BEND, 16
  An ordinary formed by two diagonal lines drawn between the upper dexter and the lower sinister sides of the shield.

BEZANT
  Flat piece of gold.

BICAPITATED, 20
  Double-headed.

ferently than the rest of the body.

Said of a fish swimming toward the dexter, its head toward the base.

Tincture (nonanimal fur) with a pattern formed of small shields arranged in horizontal lines in such a fashion that the bases of those in the upper line are opposed to the bases of the line beneath. (*See also* Counter-vair.)

Green.

Habited, clothed.

VISOR
Movable front piece of a helmet.

VOIDED
Pierced, or with some part of the charge removed, showing the field.

VULNED
Bleeding from a self-inflicted wound; said of the pelican.

Applied to wavelike line of partition, represented generally by three risings.